Jeffrey Bernard is Unwell

A play by
KEITH WATERHOUSE
based on the life and writings of
Jeffrey Bernard

Samuel French - London
New York - Toronto - Hollywood

FOR AMATEUR PRODUCTION ENQUIRIES

UNITED KINGDOM AND WORLD EXCLUDING NORTH AMERICA

plays@SamuelFrench-London.co.uk

020 7255 4302/01

Each title is subject to availability from Samuel French,

depending upon country of performance.

JEFFREY BERNARD IS UNWELL

Presented by Michael Redington at the Apollo Theatre, London, on 18th October, 1989, with the following cast of characters:

Jeffrey Bernard   Peter O'Toole

Poets	
Hacks	
Wives	
Girlfriends	
Thespians	
Publicans	
Sinners	
Policemen	
Waiters	played by:
Friends	Timothy Ackroyd
Neighbours	Sarah Berger
Jockeys	Annabel Leventon
Trainers	Royce Mills
Bores	
Artists	
Doctors	
Nurses	
Customs and Excise Officials	
Magistrate	
Drunks	
Tarts	

Directed by Ned Sherrin
Settings by John Gunter
Costumes by Stephen Brimson-Lewis

The play is set in the *Coach and Horses*, Soho, London

Time—the present, with excursions into the past

PRODUCTION NOTE

The frequent entrances and exits of the various characters are not usually indicated in the stage directions. The characters may enter and exit from any point except the street door, which remains ostentatiously locked throughout.

For the sake of pace, many of the "one-liners" in the London production were delivered from a serving hatch with a sliding door over the bar. Others were delivered as simple crossover lines as the characters crossed to any one of six exit points.

Plays by Keith Waterhouse and Willis Hall
published by Samuel French Ltd:

All Things Bright and Beautiful
Billy Liar
Celebration
Children's Day
Say Who You Are
Sponge Room *and* Squat Betty
Who's Who
Whoops-a-Daisy
Worzel Gummidge

ACT I

The set is the "Coach and Horses" pub in Soho. Getting on towards dawn
As the CURTAIN *rises, the stage is in darkness*
The poet, Elizabeth Smart, appears in a spot

Smart
My dear Jeff,
I can't say enough
how much I admire
the way you have
conducted your entire
life, and the way you have
used your marvellous Muse.
And how right she was to
choose you. Because
she's a Rare Bird who would
have retired or died
if you hadn't known how
to amuse
her, and her you
That's one non-bogus
marriage made
on Parnassus
and *true*.

She knew
exactly what and who
she was letting herself
in for: the real You.
Drink, betting shops and pubs
are the sort of thing that rubs
her up the right way;
she'll always stay
and make you more beautiful
and witty
every day.

This is a loose love
Ode, owed
to one of my friends
who is in my special
collection of people
who make amends

for endless excruciating
boring hours
so often lived
when foolishly pursuing
stimulation,
and none occurs.
Sterne, Benchley, Leacock
Carroll, and Nash, and Lear
are not more dear
to me than bedrock
Bernard . . .

Her voice fades as we lose the spot

Pause. Then a groan, a stirring, and the sound of a head hitting a piece of furniture in the darkness

Jeff Shit!

Another pause as he searches his pockets for matches. Finding a box, he uptips it in the dark

Fuck.

But finally he finds one of the spilled matches on the floor, strikes it, and finds that he is lying under a pub table. As the match goes out we hear him blundering about until he switches on a single wall light. He is in shirtsleeves and has been using his jacket for a pillow. He picks up the jacket, brushes it down, and puts it on. Lighting a cigarette, he crosses unsteadily to the street door and tries to open it. Then he looks up at the pub clock.

Five in the morning. Mark you, that's pub time. It's only ten to really . . .

He rattles the door ineffectively then, switching on another light, goes behind the bar and is about to pour himself a large vodka when he pauses

(*Crying feebly*) Help . . . ! (*Pouring the vodka*) And answer came there none, as they say in the saloon bars. So nobody can say I didn't try to get out . . . Still, there are worse places to find yourself locked in for the night than a pub, I suppose. I know a bloke who woke up at dawn in the back stalls of a cinema in Dover. All he could remember was a poster for *High Noon* in the foyer and the fact that he'd got married at twelve o'clock the previous day in the Marylebone Road Registry Office. He's divorced now. He can't even bring his ex-wife's name to mind but he does remain a very great fan of Gary Cooper . . .

He sits on a bar stool, nursing his drink, and broods for a while

At least the *Coach and Horses* has a roof. One night, when I was working on the *Sporting Life*, I woke up in a field outside Pontefract and I still have no idea how I got there. Come to that, I've no idea how I got here. I must have come in for the one, then gone down to the bog and crashed out till well after closing time, then I suppose I came back up here for the other one and quietly dozed off. It does happen. Another time when I was on the *Sporting Life* I remember opening my eyes to find myself in bed with Barry Brogan—a great jockey, true, but not my idea of a desirable bed companion. Then, on yet another occasion, I wasn't on the *Sporting Life* any longer.

The entrances and exits of the various characters who populate Jeff's life are not indicated. They appear as required and then fade back into the shadows

Editor Dear Mr Bernard, It will come as no surprise to you that following your unpardonable exhibition at the point-to-point dinner, which you attended as a representative of the *Sporting Life* on Friday evening, it is no longer possible for you to continue in our employ . . .

Jeff Oh, God. I was supposed to be making a speech—something I'd never done before. I was so nervous, I went down to the *Sporting Life* office at crack of dawn to work on it. Smithfield Market was open, so I thought if I had a couple of drinks to get me going I'd probably write rather a good one.

Editor . . . This was not, you will agree, the first time your behaviour has compromised us, and to protect myself and all connected with the *Sporting Life* from further embarrassment, I have no alternative but to terminate your engagement forthwith . . .

Jeff I drank steadily from six in the morning to seven in the evening, at which time I arrived at the hotel where I was proposing to speak and immediately passed out. Two waiters had to carry me upstairs and put me to bed.

Editor . . . I am sorry this has become necessary, but you will agree you were given every chance. I would be obliged if you would return to me your metal Press badge at your earliest convenience. Yours faithfully, Editor, *Sporting Life*.

Jeff From the Jeffrey Bernard collection of letters from the editor. Some people are in the habit of writing angry letters to the Press. I get it the other way round. The Press is in the habit of writing angry letters to me.

Kington Dear Jeffrey, Are you going to do the fucking article or aren't you? Yours, Miles Kington, Literary Editor, *Punch*.

Jeff One day I was asked to write my autobiography and I put a letter in the *Spectator* asking if anyone could tell me what I was doing between nineteen sixty and nineteen seventy-four.

Molloy Dear Mr Bernard, I read with interest your letter asking for information as to your behaviour and whereabouts between the years nineteen sixty to nineteen seventy-four. On a certain evening in September nineteen sixty-nine, you rang my mother to inform her that you were going to murder her only son. If you would like further information, I can put you in touch with many people who have enjoyed similar bizarre experiences in your company. Yours sincerely, Michael J. Molloy, Editor, *Daily Mirror*.

Jeff goes behind the bar and pours himself another stiff vodka

Jeff I could die here. It's a good thing I can hold this stuff tolerably well. I mean, if I were a yob or a Hurrah Henry, by the time the pub opens again

I could be one of those cases found by the coroner to have choked on their own vomit. Disgusting phrase. When did you hear of anyone choking on someone else's vomit? I'm putting these on the slate, by the way. I don't believe in freeloading.

Carrying his drink, he comes round from behind the bar and prowls around the pub

Dear Sir, May I add a few words to your excellent obituary of Jeffrey Bernard who has regrettably died from choking. I knew him intimately for over fifty years and I feel that many of his more remarkable qualities were left unsung in your otherwise comprehensive review of his messy life. He was born in nineteen thirty-two—probably by mistake—covered from head to foot in eczema. One of the first things he did was to wet the bed and he continued to do so until he was fifteen. A weak, thin-skinned and over-sensitive boy, he had few friends at school. He usually chose to sit at the very back of the classroom so that he could play with himself unobserved. His early obsession with sex prevented him from obtaining any worthwhile academic honours. By the time he left school he had become a chain smoker and compulsive writer of fan letters to Veronica Lake.

In nineteen forty-six he paid his first visit to Soho and from that point he was never to look forward. It was here in the cafés and pubs of Dean Street and Old Compton Street that he was to develop his remarkable sloth, envy and self-pity. It was about this time we began to realize that Jeffrey was not cut out for a career as a naval officer as his mother had hoped.

He drifted from job to job and, between jobs, he spent months at a time accepting small sums of money from homosexuals and friends. He began to develop a greed for unearned money and the growing conviction that he was cut out for better things. After a short, undistinguished spell in the army, from which he was given a medical discharge with his pay-book marked "Mental stability nil", he returned to Soho, got married for the first time out of four, and split up with his wife a few weeks later.

It was during this period that he first became involved with horse-racing and gambling, and the feelings of infantile omnipotence, that this activity prompted were to last him for the rest of his life. These feelings were particularly noticeable in his dealings with women and some even said that his life was a never-ending cliché of a search for his mother. His drinking began to escalate to such an extent that he was unable to hold down the most ordinary of jobs and he was consequently advised to take up journalism. Even in this field he was never offered a staff appointment, and he gradually drifted into writing a series of personal and, at times, embarrassing columns about his own wretched experiences.

After a spell in the alcohol and drug-addiction unit at St Bernard's Hospital (no relation), Hanwell, he developed the fantasy that, starting tomorrow, it would all be different. My last memory of Bernard is of seeing him staring at his typewriter and fighting yet another battle against his chronic amnesia. He leaves two unwritten books and a circle of detached acquaintances.

His perambulations have taken him back to the bar where there is a telephone. He is about to pick it up when his extemporized self-obituary reminds him

Did you know, by the way, there's a bloke in America who sells talking tombstones? Before someone pegs out, as it might be a wife, they record a message on tape, then, when the husband comes to put a jar of dandelions on her grave on Sunday, he presses a button and lo, it's the same old story again.

Wife So there you are. I'm amazed you managed to tear yourself away from the pub. Your dinner's in the oven. You're drunk again, aren't you? You make me sick. Honestly, I thought you'd change and settle down. Don't you ever think of the future? Christ, this headache's killing me. And stop staring at that women in the next grave. You needn't bother to come next Sunday. I'll be all right. Don't worry about me—you never did before so why start now? Always thinking of yourself. Me, me, me. Good-bloody-bye and where do you think you're taking those flowers? You make me sick!

Jeff picks up the receiver

Jeff I'll try giving old Norman a bell. The landlord—maybe he'll come and bail me out. Old Norman. He likes being called old Norman, that's why I do it, sycophant that I am. He slings down a vodka, snarls "There you are, get your own fucking ice, haven't you got anything smaller?" and we all say good old Norman. Fancies himself as a "bit of a character". Most landlords do, have you noticed? And if they're not bits of characters themselves, they know plenty of people who are . . .

Forgetting his phone call for the time being, he puts the receiver down

One time when I was working as a barman, the publican was one of those dreadful men who call you "squire" and think of themselves as "your genial host". On my first day, he came up to me where I was polishing the Smirnoff bottle and said——

Landlord You see that bloke going out? Now *he's* a bit of a character.

Jeff (*yawning*) Oh, yes? Well, Guvnor, you mustn't keep me from my work.

Landlord Yes. Would you believe that man must lose at least six umbrellas a year?

Jeff Well, well. (*Resuming his narrative*) I mean, I know the shortage of eccentrics is acute these days, but you'd think a pub landlord of all people could come up with someone slightly more interesting than an umbrella loser. Even I can do better than that. For instance, an antique dealer I know who was once voted Rat of the Week by the old *Sunday Pictorial*, a doctor who's had a cold for five years, and an ex-embassy press attaché who now writes the flagellation column for a seedy magazine, and that's just off the top of my head.

He picks up the telephone again, is about to dial, then remembers something else

Dennis Shaw. Does that name mean anything? Now there *was* a character. The face that closed a thousand cinemas. He used to play villains and Gestapo men in those wonderfully-awful British B pictures. Twenty stone and encrusted in warts—imagine a toad wearing a dinner jacket and that was Dennis Shaw, or Den-Den as he called himself. One night that dear, sweet man John Le Mesurier—now there was another character—one night, John Le Mes was walking along Piccadilly when he saw Dennis Shaw being bundled into a Black Maria for drunk and disorderly. John Le Mes gave him one of his affable smiles and said——

John Le Mes Hello, Dennis. Working?

Jeff He must have been drunker and even more disorderly than usual because the police didn't like taking him in very much, as I found once when I tried to get him arrested for being boring. He'd gatecrashed my table in a restaurant and thoroughly spoiled my dinner by just sitting there being Dennis Shaw, then he got into my cab and wouldn't get out so I made the driver take us to Tottenham Court Road police station. Whereupon, he bounded into the nick, reappearing a moment later with four policemen and booming——

Shaw Gentlemen, I'd like you to meet Jeffrey Bernard, the biggest idiot in Soho.

Jeff He then sat down on the pavement and refused to budge. But all the desk sergeant said was——

Sergeant We'd rather not arrest Mr Shaw, sir, if you don't mind. He's a bit difficult in the cells, you see.

Jeff One night I was out on the piss with Den-Den—a rather difficult enterprise, considering he was barred from every pub within a six-mile radius of Charing Cross—and we finished up in the *Stork Club* where we went through the card. Dinner, the full works, a bottle of champagne for me and a bottle of Gordon's gin for Den-Den. Now, I'd been paying all evening and in any case the bugger owed me for enough dinners to feed the five thousand, so when the bill came I refrained from picking it up. So did Den-Den. After a while the waiters started stacking chairs on the tables and after another while the cleaners arrived and started vacuuming the floor, but still we sat there finishing Den-Den's gin with the bill untouched and unread on the table. Finally, the head waiter came over and even in the cold, grey light of dawn you could see his face turn white as he saw who it was.

By now Jeff and Shaw are sitting at a table

Waiter Good-morning, Mr Shaw.
Shaw So you remember me.
Waiter I do indeed, Mr Shaw.
Shaw Tell this gentleman where we last met.
Waiter At the *Pigalle*, Mr Shaw, when I was head waiter there.
Shaw Under what circumstances did we become acquainted?

Waiter You refused to pay your bill, Mr Shaw.
Shaw Tell this gentleman what your response was to that.
Waiter I called the police, Mr Shaw.
Shaw (*thumping the table*) Call the bastards again!
Jeff (*rising*) He was a collector's item, was Den-Den. And never lost an
umbrella in his life. He found quite a few, though.

He crosses to the telephone again. Lighting a cigarette, he finally dials

(*After a while*) He's got to be home, so he must be out for the count. I
wonder if I put a call through the engineers whether they could somehow
make it ring louder . . .

*Cradling the phone on his shoulder, he idly picks up a discarded copy of "The
Times" from a bar stool*

(*After reading for a moment*) I think this has been left here for my benefit.
One of those crappy features on the subject of alcoholism . . .

*Putting the paper down again, he jiggles the telephone receiver impatiently
against his ear*

Whatever the opposite of insomnia is, Norman has got it. An enviable
talent. The only time I get a good sleep is face down in the blueberry pie
over lunch at the *Groucho Club* . . .

*Giving up on his phone call he replaces the receiver and picks up "The Times"
again*

"Have you a drinking problem?"—the usual list of odd questions, and if
you answer yes, it shows there's "serious cause for alarm". The trouble is,
the more I look at these questions the less alarmed I feel. In fact, I've just
this minute come to the conclusion that I don't drink enough . . .

He moves behind the bar where he pours himself another stiff one

I wish someone'd pay *me* to write a quiz on boozing—I'd be laughing all
the way to the *Groucho* . . . I wonder if they'd pay me to supply the
answers?

"The Times" Questioner is a very starchy, disapproving-looking lady

Questioner Do you have time off from work because of drinking, or has
your work performance suffered because of alcohol?
Jeff The situation is very much the reverse. Work frequently interferes with
my drinking. Besides, drinking *is* my work. I was once paid five hundred
pounds for an article on this very subject.
Questioner Do your family——
Jeff Just a minute, I haven't finished. I'll have you know I once fired my
agent for being pissed all the time. I told her, "One of us has to be sober,
and it isn't going to be me."
Questioner Have there been family quarrels because of your drinking?
Jeff I believe there was a tremendous row in nineteen thirty-four as to
whether I should be fed Nestlés or Cow and Gate.

Questioner And are you becoming difficult, irritable and testy after drinking?

Jeff You must be joking. I'm impossible. After closing time last Tuesday I hit a Greek greengrocer in Goodge Street who asked me not to feel his cucumbers.

Questioner Do you find your memory is getting worse?

Jeff Could you repeat the question?

Questioner Have you ever had loss of memory after a heavy drinking session?

Jeff Quite honestly I can't remember ever having had a heavy drinking session.

Questioner Do you order yourself a double when the rest of your party are drinking singles, or do you order yourself a quick extra drink while collecting an order from the bar?

Jeff None of my "party" drinks singles. They do have some style, you know. As to ordering a quick drink, I can tell you there's no such thing in this fucking place. It takes longer to get a drink in here than it takes to get a refund out of the Inland Revenue.

Questioner Has your sexual drive and ability suffered because of your drinking?

Jeff Mind your own fucking business.

Questioner And finally, do you——?

Jeff Sorry—no more questions. It'll soon be opening time in Billingsgate.

Questioner You make me sick!

Jeff speaks confidentially as the Questioner departs

Jeff In fact, I didn't want to say this in front of *The Times*, but owing to some tablets I've been taking in conjunction with a small port, to which I am not accustomed—that's what drunk chartered accountants always claim when hauled up at Bow Street—I find myself on the verge of suffering from impotence, or incompetence as some women call it. Though suffering's the wrong word—impotence has its drawbacks: like you stand no chance of being held down and raped by three nubile girls, which is what once happened to a bloke on Malibu Beach and the next night you couldn't see the sea for the entire male population of Southern California. But it's not in the least uncommon, you know. There are fifty-five thousand impotent men in the Avon and Somerset area alone—that's what I read in the *Daily Telegraph*. I wonder how they know. Were they shopped to the medical authorities by fifty-five thousand disgruntled women? And why is the West Country so heavily afflicted? Could it be the cider? No—apparently the causes of impotence are given as stemming from diabetes, alcohol, pelvic injuries, drugs and psychological problems. (*Lighting a cigarette*) If smoking sixty of these things a day counts as a drug then I'm holding a full house for the first time since I played poker in the army. But I personally welcome impotence and wish it would hurry up and come, so to speak. I raise my glass to it, though not much else. What a release—for the first time since the age of fourteen, when I formed an ambition to be a sex object instead of a good seam bowler, I will no longer be led about by my prick. When I ponder the fact that my life lies in ruins solely because I have always followed the direction in which my various erections were pointing, I wish to God I'd been born a girl. Which reminds me. In the steam bath one day I found Solly, a seventy-year-old taxi driver, staring at his private member and moaning——

Solly We were born together. We grew up together. We went courting together. We got married together. We had children together. Why, oh why, oh why did you have to die before me?

Jeff Another of the delights of impotence is that I should set fire to the bed a bit less often. You see, I am somewhat in the habit of being asked for cigarettes by ladies while lying in my bed. Not after the event—that's always been the man's prerogative—but before it. Usually what's happened is that I've jumped the gun by getting into bed in the belief I was being followed. But what these ladies do is light up a cigarette and then give you a hundred specious reasons for having to go home.

1st Girl My husband may be phoning from Paris.

2nd Girl My cat can't bear to be left alone.

3rd Girl But we've only known each other for a day . . .

4th Girl Half a day . . .

5th Girl Half an hour . . .

6th Girl The baby-sitter will go mad if I'm late.

7th Girl But people simply don't *do* it in broad daylight, do they?

Jeff One more advantage, by the way. Not having to wrestle with one-liners like those any more means not having to put up with one-liners like these any more, after they've moved in.

1st Girl And where do you think you're going?

2nd Girl You've been drinking.

3rd Girl Can we go home now, please?

4th Girl Your dinner's in the oven.

5th Girl You make me sick.

Jeff But to get back to the bedside manner . . .

8th Girl I like you, Jeff, I like you a lot. But not in that way.

Jeff So. I resign myself to the situation, take a Valium, fall asleep with the last fag in my mouth and wake up to find the bedspread in flames. I started keeping a fire extinguisher by my bed but I never really knew whether to aim it at the mattress, the lady—if she was still there—or my private parts.

Once more he crosses to the telephone, picks it up and dials

(*After listening for a while*) Maybe he's taken a Valium too. Perhaps I should call the fire brigade . . . Come on, Norman, some of us have got homes to go to, as you landlords so often remind us . . . (*Recollecting with a frown*) Though now that I come to think about it, some of us haven't.

He replaces the telephone and, during the following, brings out a suitcase and a couple of carrier bags, stuffed with possessions, from behind the bar where they have been stored

Women again. Why haven't they got labels on their heads saying "Danger, Government health warning: women can seriously damage your brains, genitals, current account, confidence, razor blades and good standing among your friends"? Sometimes they walk out on you, sometimes they throw you out, all depending on whose bed you were in when you set it on fire. This was a throwing-out job. At least I was allowed access to my worldly goods. Love locked out is one thing, but when it's love plus your books and Mozart tapes, all your spare clothes and shoes, plus your framed photograph of yourself with Lester Piggott, it can be well nigh unbearable while it lasts.

Rummaging among his belongings he locates the Lester Piggott picture and puts it on a table

No-one would ever call Lester a laugh a minute but don't let anybody tell you he has no sense of humour. He even sends up his own legendary meanness. There's a story about the time years and years ago when he'd ridden another winner and the stable lad was kept waiting for the customary tip.

Lad Excuse me, Lester, but do you think you could drop me a pound for that winner I did you?

Piggott (*cocking a hand to his ear*) What?

Lad That winner I did you. You were going to drop me a pound.

Piggott Can't hear you. That's my bad ear.

Lad (*close up to the other ear*) What about a couple of quid for that winner I did for you?

Piggott Still can't hear. Try the one pound ear again.

Rummaging again, after a reflective moment, Jeff unearths a bundle of letters and riffles through them

Jeff Some letters tied with barbed wire. I don't know why I bother keeping them. Or why they bother writing them. They're all identical.

Mistress Dear Jeffrey, It was madness from the start. You must have known as well as I did that it could never work. Why on earth did we ever start it? Your moods crushed me. I put out a hand, but you never took it. Well, you did take. My God, that's all you ever did—take, take, take. You say you like women, but I really think you hate them. Not once did you ever listen to me when I wanted to talk about me. You were just waiting for me to stop talking and get my clothes off. Then, in that Chinese restaurant in Gerrard Street, you finally did it. You insulted everything I hold sacred. The family unit. Carshalton Beeches. *Cosmopolitan*, and money. No, I'm sorry, it's all over. I hope you find true happiness, as I have.

Jeff No doubt with a film-maker aged about thirty who drives a Ferrari coupé with one bronze arm leaning nonchalantly over the offside door, and who lives in a riverside penthouse with a Burmese cat, several gold medallions, a bottle of after shave, an extremely expensive hi-fi set and no self-doubt whatsoever.

Mistress PS. You make me sick.

Jeff She could have been the fifth Mrs Bernard if I'd played my cards wrong. Trouble was, she had the most extraordinary ideas about what's called "settling down". This is a very curious phrase used only by women. I've seen feathered birds settling down and I've seen dust settling down and I've seen bookmakers settling *up* even, but what do all these women mean by settling down? I suspect they mean that life is no laughing matter. You could have fooled me. But what puzzles me is what on earth did my four wives think they were getting when they married me? I mean, you can see a train when it's coming. But they thought I'd change and settle down.

He unearths framed photographs of himself with various ladies and displays them on one of the pub tables

As a matter of fact, I think I *have* settled down insofar as I'm pretty set in my ways. I have come to terms with the fact that my dinner is in the oven and always will be. I have also learned to accept the fact that——

Bore You only get out of life what you put into it.

Jeff The sagacious prick who gave me that piece of information would have had his teeth knocked out if I hadn't been in an alcoholic and diabetic coma at the time, but he meant well. And bless my soul, don't the ladies mean well when they ask you to change and settle down? Never trust people who mean well. Hitler probably meant well and Cromwell certainly hoped we'd change and settle down.

Anyway, I was tremendously flattered when this girl said to me——

Mistress When I first saw you in the pub I thought to myself, what's this handsome man doing surrounded by rogues?

Jeff Apart from her suspect eyesight, she's answered her own question, if you see what I mean. Surrounded by rogues. Say no more. But for her, I'd try to change and settle down. "Darling, I've asked a few rogues to Sunday lunch. No Knickers Joyce says she'll weed the border, Maltese Laurie's going to mow the lawn and Norman says he'll carve the joint. We could play bridge in the evening and perhaps we might splash out on a bottle of sherry."

Mistress "Oh, Jeffrey, you're an absolute poppet. I'm so glad you've changed and settled down. You don't miss Soho and all those awful people, do you, darling?"

Jeff "Of course not, my angel. Take your knickers off. Oops, sorry. Forgot. We're married and settled down in Chislehurst."

Jeff finds in his belongings a photograph of the Mistress. Smoking pensively, he sets it on a table of its own and looks at it reflectively

But if I never change, neither do they. When they leave you, for instance. I wonder who writes their scripts?

Mistress It's over. You've snapped at me for the last time. As far as I'm concerned, anything there was is finished.

Jeff (*still narrating*) I can't say I was surprised but I still couldn't get on to her wavelength. You might know that strange thought process. It's got nothing to do with arrogance or conceit—simply a dull amazement at the fact that someone can't see how truly wonderful you are. I mean, there you are, standing right in front of them, the never-to-be-repeated offer of a lifetime, in your prime and only a short climb away from your peak, and the fools can't see it. It never fails to amaze me.

Mistress I don't mind going to the cinema with you, or going dutch for a meal—but so far as anything else is concerned, it's over.

Jeff She waited for me to say something. I stood there thinking of about six different things at once.

Mistress Aren't you going to say anything?

Jeff I couldn't. I was miles away. That business about going dutch had really got me. I had a vision of us drifting in and out of cinemas and restaurants, and me—or worse still, her—always saying to the management——

Mistress Do you mind if we have separate bills? You see, I don't sleep with him any more.

Jeff Also, I was thinking how very hard she was going to be to replace. She still stood staring at me, her brown eyes flecked with malice and realistic thinking.

Mistress Well?

Jeff I still couldn't think of anything to say memorable enough to haunt her for the rest of her days, so I put on my mask of tragedy and went through the usual motions of offering up the late, late prayer. It's one all hopeless punters mutter in betting shops and it goes——

Punter Please, God, let's start again. I know I've been a fool, but if this horse wins the last race I promise I'll never have another bet again. Ever.

Jeff But it doesn't work with women. Come to that, it doesn't work with horses either.

Mistress Very well . . .

Jeff Suddenly I saw that picture from my schooldays of Napoleon on the deck of the *Bellerophon* saying farewell to Europe—only it wasn't Napoleon, it was me. Actually, more post Charing Cross than post Waterloo so far as I was concerned. I was upset, yes—no-one likes their sweets taken away—but I wasn't heartbroken.

Mistress So it's goodbye, then.

Jeff Then she shrugged her mouth and left. I found myself thinking: it's just like they say it is in novels. Women really do turn on their heels when they go. I watched her down the stairs and heard the front door close and then I heard her nasty, tinny little Renault starting up below. I waited for her to crash the gears but she didn't. It's bloody fantastic, I thought while I made some tea. After a scene like that she remains so icy cold that for once she doesn't make a mess of the gears. I mean, I ask you—would a man remain so utterly cool after closing a rhapsodical chapter in his life? Not him—he'd drive straight into a wall blinded by tears at a moderately safe fifteen miles an hour and she'd come running down the stairs and out into the street deliciously blaming herself.

The sound of screeching brakes. Jeff smiles malevolently

That's better. I took my cup of tea into the sitting-room and sat there wondering at my own coolness. I felt quite ashamed at not being more upset so I put some Mahler on to see if he could provoke the appropriate misery. Nothing. In fact, I sat there listening to the syrup feeling distinctly irritated. She'd be on the phone now, I reckoned, to an old, reliable friend.

As we bring up the Mahler the Old Reliable Friend, filling his pipe, enters and sits at a table with a bottle of wine, where he is joined by the Mistress

God, how I hate those old, reliable, pipe-smoking friends who, of course, have never laid a finger on the lady in question—they lecture at some obscure university on Anglo-Saxon pottery and you can't get more decent than that. The bugger's just been waiting for her affair to go on the rocks. Up until then he's been hanging around like a non-functioning lighthouse but now he suddenly lights up.

Mistress No, actually, I was very fond of him, Bob.

Jeff They've always got old, reliable names like Bob.

Mistress It's just that he needs more love than I can possibly give him.

Old Reliable I know, darling, I know . . .

Jeff . . . says Bob, patting her hand while at the same time catching the wine waiter's eye, filling his pipe with St Bruno, grinding the pepper mill over madam's artichoke and scribbling a note about a new find of sixth-century cocoa mugs near Winchester.

Mistress I really was very attached to him. It's just that I couldn't take any more of his eternal snapping.

Old Reliable I know, I know. But you must have known it couldn't last.

Jeff They always say that. I wonder they don't set themselves up as bloody fortune-tellers.

Old Reliable I could tell he was trouble from the moment I set eyes on him, but, of course, one doesn't like to pour cold water on love's young dream.

Jeff How about throwing up on it, then? So, after plying her with wine he wastes a good dinner by pouring her into a taxi with the words——

Old Reliable What you need, my dear, is a good night's sleep. Now you just try to forget all about him.

Mistress (*pecking his cheek*) Dear Bob. I don't know what I'd do without you.

Jeff All that happened a long time ago. I haven't seen her since; the Mahler's well-scratched by now and I've licked my wounds clean . . . Then two weeks ago she had the cheek to ring me up and ask me if I happened to know of a good plumber. Some people have no sensitivity whatsoever.

Delving into his belongings, Jeff produces a pair of tortoiseshell-backed hairbrushes

(*Staring at them*) Tortoiseshell hairbrushes. Now how did I acquire these? I know. In settlement of a bad debt by a very severe case of alopecia. (*A moment's brooding*) I wonder what it's like to be a tortoise. Not a barrel of laughs, I shouldn't imagine. You can't be frivolous or facetious if you're a

tortoise, can you? And think of the danger of being turned into a pair of hairbrushes. But you do have a home to go to. Just pull in your head and there you are, all snug and cosy . . . God, I hate flat-hunting. And I hate staying with other people while I'm looking for somewhere to live. No matter how kind and generous they are, you can see them looking at you all the time, with their eyes pleading——
Host Please, please, Jeff, don't get pissed and set the flat on fire.
Jeff One thing I know. I will never ever again live anywhere beyond staggering distance of the *Coach and Horses*.

During the following, he produces photographs from his belongings, looking at them and setting them up on the pub tables

I pitched my tent in Soho at around thirteen and it's been a downhill struggle ever since. And if anyone wonders how such a dump could possibly have gripped me and seduced me, then they didn't know Soho when you could end up drunk, penniless and alone on less than a pound. To step out of both the classroom and my mother's Dresden-littered drawing-room into this enchanted dungheap was like waking up in Disneyland, Treasure Island, Pleasure Island, you name it. And what an incredible mixture I've had the luck to stumble across, mostly in the gutter where you find the best company. Poets, painters, prostitutes, bookies' runners, bohemians, bums, philosophers, crooks, cranks. Dylan Thomas, Francis Bacon, Lucien Freud, John Minton, Frank Norman, French Vera, No Knickers Joyce, Sid the Swimmer, Ironfoot Jack, Nina Hamnett, Muriel Belcher. Muriel Belcher! She ran the *Colony Room Club* or Muriel's as it was always known. I can see her now, sitting on her stool at the end of the bar, like a raven on its perch, and chatting up the punters.
Muriel Come on, cunty, spend up. You're not buying enough champagne. Are you a member, sir? Go on, then, fuck off. Members only.
Jeff She did have her favourites, though. There was a charming old queen who worked in the City and drank Scotch for England at Muriel's every evening. He was more or less a club hostess but it happened that he'd won the Military Cross in nineteen sixteen when he was a captain in the Guards, and whenever anyone asked Muriel why she put up with him, she always said——
Muriel She was a very brave little woman at the Somme.
Jeff There was this bearded bugger, well known for his compulsive verbosity. One afternoon he walked into Muriel's and said——
Bore Muriel, I'm worried. I've got to got to a fancy-dress party tonight and I can't think what to go as.
Muriel Why don't you put talc on your chin and go as an armpit?
Jeff Of course, it was all too good to miss a moment of, so working for a living was out of the question. I did the odd job obligatory in the life of a bum—navvying, dishwashing, acting, even a spell down a coal mine and then in a boxing booth in a fairground. But I was always drawn back to Soho who was always there waiting with open arms and legs.

He takes out a collection of tapes from one of his carrier bags and browses through them

Rosenkavalier. That must be when I was working at Covent Garden as a sceneshifter. Do you know—the flymen and sceneshifters at the Royal Opera House are the most discriminating critics you could wish to meet. I'd trust their judgement rather than those long-haired prats on Radio Three any day.

We hear a snatch of "Der Rosenkavalier"

Sceneshifter Tell you what, Jeff. (*Spitting*) I don't care who she is—I've shit better Rosenkavaliers than this one.

Jeff broods through the rest of the snatch until the music fades

Jeff I now realize it's highly likely that the two biggest of the many mistakes I've made in my life were to have moved from Soho to Suffolk in nineteen sixty-six and from Soho to Berkshire in nineteen seventy-eight, both times with new wives, in the pathetic belief that geographical change would solve all my problems. But any idea that living in the country is romantic is all romancing so far as I'm concerned. The idyll is utterly without stimulus and all those trees and all that grass drain the spirit. I remember once foolishly suggesting to Francis Bacon that he could solve all his tax headaches by moving to Switzerland.

Bacon Are you crazy? All those fucking views—they'd drive me mad.

Jeff And it's not only the views—it's the dreadful horsebrassy pubs run by rude, jumped-up shopkeepers in blazers and cravats, and it's the bloody regulars—the Backbone of England and his lady wife, Mrs Backbone. Of Neck of the Woods.

Mr Backbone wears an anorak, Mrs Backbone a sheepskin coat and headscarf. They come in vigorously rubbing and clapping their hands

They invariably make the same entrance wherever they go—I presume they're rehearsed in it as children. Then Mr Backbone says——

Backbone Brrrr!

Jeff And Mrs Backbone says——

Mrs Backbone Brrrr!

Jeff Then Mr Backbone says——

Backbone What'll you have, darling?

Jeff And Mrs Backbone says——

Mrs Backbone Ooh, let's see. What shall I have?

Jeff So Mr Backbone says——

Backbone Why don't you have a whisky mac?

Jeff And Mrs Backbone says——

Mrs Backbone Yes, why don't I have a whisky mac?

Jeff Good idea!

Mrs Backbone Good idea, darling. Yes, I'll have a whisky mac. What are you going to have, darling?

Jeff —asks Mrs Backbone.

Backbone Ooh, I'm not sure, darling. I know——
Jeff —says Mr Backbone.
Backbone —I think I'll have a nice bottle of Guinness.
Jeff There! Then, when Mr Backbone dips into his pocket for change he
   drops a coin on the floor and quick as a flash the barmaid says——
Barmaid Leave it for the sweeper.
Jeff Pause for laughter. Then, when the drinks have been savoured by our
   resident Bisto Kids——
Backbone Mmmmm!
Mrs Backbone Mmmmm!
Jeff —the Backbones of England smile knowingly at one another, and then
   Mr Backbone says to the barmaid——
Backbone Busy Christmas?
Jeff And the barmaid says——
Barmaid Ooh, terrible. Packed all the time we were.
Backbone Well——
Jeff —says Mr Backbone.
Backbone —that's over for another year, anyway.
Jeff And Mrs Backbone, her nose dripping in unison with his, decides it's
   time for her to scintillate.
Mrs Backbone Yes, all over for another year.
Backbone You can say that again, darling.
Jeff —says Mr Backbone, nodding approvingly at a horse-brass, and does
   so.
Backbone All over for another year.
Jeff I know, deep down, that they're going to continue to plunder the
   calendar and I should leave now but I don't. I just wait for it. And Mr
   Backbone rubs his hands and asks the Still Life with Pineapple Ice-
   bucket——
Backbone How was the New Year, then?
Barmaid New Year?
Jeff —squawks the barmaid.
Barmaid Don't talk about it.
Jeff But Mr Backbone does.
Backbone Oh, like that, was it?
Jeff And Mrs Backbone echoes——
Mrs Backbone Like that, eh?
Jeff To which she adds saucily, to Mr Backbone——
Mrs Backbone Ours was pretty hectic too, wasn't it, darling?
Backbone Always is——
Jeff —concurs Mr Backbone.
Backbone Still, you expect it, don't you?
Mrs Backbone Wouldn't be New Year if it wasn't, would it, darling?
Jeff —says Mrs Backbone, and I drink up and leave before they embark on
   their forecasts for Easter. (*He crosses towards the bar, then pauses as a
   thought strikes him*) I do have one unfulfilled ambition as regards the
   country, though. I once remarked to Fred Winter on how healthy his
   horses looked.

Winter That's because they don't sit up all night playing cards and drinking vodka.

Jeff And it occurred to me to wonder what would happen—just what would happen—if you fed into the average farm animal what some of us consume in the course of a single day. I'd very much like to wake up one morning with a cow of the Friesian variety and walk her down here to the *Coach and Horses*, stopping on the way to buy twenty Players, ply her with vodka until closing time, whip her off to an Indian restaurant, take her up to the *Colony Room* till five thirty and then on to the *York Minster*, *Swiss Tavern* and *Three Greyhounds*, get beaten up by Chinese waiters at midnight, have a row with a taxi driver, set the bed on fire, put it out with tears and then wake up on the floor. Could you then milk said cow? I doubt it.

Resuming his journey to the bar he pours himself a vodka, then picks up the phone and dials

(*Drumming his fingers impatiently*) Norman—will you please answer the bloody phone? I am locked in your pub and drinking all your vodka. And another thing—there's no ice. (*Narrating again*) Not that that'd move him, the ungracious bugger. Yesterday I asked him for the menu and he threw it at me. When he brought my cottage pie I thought he was going to throw that at me, too. Instead he said to the man sitting on that bar stool, "Get off your arse and let Jeff sit down—he's fucking ill." I am fucking ill, too. As the *Spectator* always puts it when I'm too fucking ill to write my column——

Spectator Jeffrey Bernard is unwell.

Jeff I tell a lie—they don't invariably say that. They have been known to put it another way.

Spectator Jeffrey Bernard's column does not appear this week, as it is remarkably similar to that which he wrote last week.

Jeff is by now in bed—one of the "Coach and Horses" chaise longues—being tucked in by a Nurse

Nurse Why *do* you drink so much, Mr Bernard?

Jeff To stop myself from jogging.

As the Nurse departs with a sigh, Jeff unfolds the copy of the "Sporting Life" she brought in for him. Forgetting the audience, he studies it for a while

I'm about to do you a favour. I'm going to refrain from advising you what to back in the big race tomorrow. A tip is only an opinion and I'll give you a tip—the nearer the horse's mouth it is, the more it's worth ignoring. And that goes each way.

The trouble with betting is that if you lose you lose, and if you win you think about how much more you *could* have won if you'd doubled the stake. It's pathetic, really. I think a psychiatrist I know probably hit the nail on the head when he described punting as——

Psychiatrist Collecting injustices.

Jeff This was when I was in a very curious establishment in Surrey which was like a gambling research clinic. On the third day of my confinement, the psychiatrist came along and sat down beside my bed with a great wad of papers, an instrument for measuring blood pressure, a thermometer and the *Sporting Life*. I thought he was going to delve into my childhood and establish whether I still felt guilt at introducing the sport of masturbation to my prep school—as a matter of fact I felt like Marco Polo returning to Europe with the new invention of gunpowder, and soon the whole school was rocked to its foundations both metaphorically and physically. But not a bit of it. He went straight to the point.

Psychiatrist Do you think King's Ransom has a better chance than Baby Dumpling at York this afternoon?

Jeff No. Looking at the weights, I'd say that Baby Dumpling has a better chance than King's Ransom.

Psychiatrist You really are in a bad way, my friend. King's Ransom will piss it.

Jeff He then went off to back King's Ransom and thus prove I was mad. But Baby Dumpling pissed it.

Nurse I should be careful, Mr Bernard. We had a man in here who was such a good tipster the psychiatrist kept him in for five months.

Jeff rises hastily as he continues his narrative

Jeff I became hooked on racing when I was about sixteen and doing time at a disgusting naval college called Pangbourne. A boy called Vickers got twelve of the best—the maximum—for running a book. I was deeply impressed. It put gambling in the same wicked league as drinking and sex and if it was as bad as that I wanted some of it. It took thirty-five years for retribution to set in. Not twelve of the best, but an appearance at Bow Street magistrates' court. After a long series of contributions to the Joe Coral Benevolent Fund, my luck changed or so I believed at the time. I had a yankee up and won over two grand—a big win for a small punter. It was the sort of win that compensates for all the losses but then I began to reflect that since it had taken three and a half decades to arrive at that one big win, punting was indeed a mug's game after all. So I decided to open a book. Just among friends and acquaintances, in a small, fun sort of way. But the law didn't see it quite like that and my luck changed again.

A Customs Officer has appeared. He speaks in the sing-song tones of one giving evidence in court

Customs Officer On thirteenth of June, at approximately fourteen hundred hours, I entered the *Coach and Horses* public house, Greek Street, London W1, as an officer of Customs and Excise. A television set was switched on showing racing from Sandown and York. A man who I now know to be Jeffrey Bernard said——

Jeff Does anyone want anything on this?

There are now other people standing around the bar

Customs Officer —just as the three o'clock race from Sandown was starting. I asked a woman at the bar for the running number of a horse called Bonhomie. She consulted her newspaper and replied. At this point, Mr Bernard said to me——

Jeff Do you want a bet?

Customs Officer I handed him two one pound coins and asked for Bonhomie. Two other customers handed Mr Bernard coins and both asked for Bonhomie. Mr Bernard turned to a female companion and said——

Jeff If Bonhomie wins I'm fucked.

Customs Officer Bonhomie lost and I left the premises at approximately fifteen eighteen hours.

One of the customers at the bar proves to be a Customs Investigator. He draws up two chairs facing one another

Investigator Would you care to sit down, Mr Bernard? Just a few questions ... (*He flashes his identity card*) Now do you pay tax to the government on these bets you've been taking?

Jeff How could I? I'm not a licensed bookmaker.

Investigator Do you think it's against the law not to pay tax?

Jeff I do now.

Investigator Why do the regulars bet with you rather than go to the Mecca around the corner?

Jeff They regard it as fun and are too lazy to walk to the betting shop and desert their drinks. It's a joke between us. I think they're fools and they think I'm one. We're taking the piss out of one another.

Investigator Do they bet with you because you don't charge tax?

Jeff No, it's just a game. Nobody's that mean—at least, my friends aren't.

Investigator How well do you have to know someone before you take bets off them?

Jeff They'd have to be friends or acquaintances, not strangers. Most of them are good mates.

Investigator Would you be surprised to know you've accepted bets from customs officers?

Jeff (*to himself*) Fuck.

Rising, he resumes his narrative

It took nine policemen and three customs men in one wagon and one squad car to arrest me. Little me. At how much public expense I don't know, but they recovered the vital sum of thirty-one pounds twelve pence in evaded betting tax.

Magistrate Anything known?

Jeff (*still narrating*) Not a lot. I was once nicked for going over the top with a rubber plant in the *Raj of India* restaurant. Then I collected another bit of a criminal record for kicking someone's car parked annoyingly on the pavement. A CID man arrested me here in the *Coach and Horses* and took me to Vine Street to be fingerprinted and photographed. But here's an

extraordinary thing. *As we were walking past a certain pub on our way to the nick, the detective suddenly said——*
Detective You screwed the landlord's daughter here in nineteen seventy-six, didn't you?
Jeff I was amazed. How anyone but me and the party of the second part could have knowledge of what went on that Christmas Day on the saloon-bar floor when the guvnor went upstairs for his after-lunch nap, I'll never know. But I liked the magistrate. He looked up my previous form and said——
Magistrate The last time it was rubber plants, Mr Bernard. Now it's cars. What next?
Jeff Keeping a book without paying betting tax, that's what's next.
Magistrate Quite. Fined two hundred pounds and fifty pounds costs.
Jeff Ah, well. A mere fleabite compared with what the sods did to Lester Piggott and as we always say around here, if you can't take a joke you shouldn't have joined.

He opens his suitcase, rummages about in it and produces a clean but crumpled shirt which he holds up for inspection

Oh, dear. When Norman finally does surface he's going to think I look more dishevelled even than after that night I spent in the ditch of the celebrated Pond Fence at Sandown. I don't know how I got there, or who my companion was, but we got on famously.

Tossing the shirt on a chair he moves off with uncertain step—for the first time showing signs of drunkenness—to a back room where we hear him crashing and banging about. Unseen by Jeff, a folded page of the "Spectator" has fallen out of the shirt pocket and now lies on the floor. Elizabeth Smart enters and stands motionless in the same spot as formerly. Jeff staggers out of the back room with an ironing board and an iron

(*Trying to set up the ironing board*) People are always surprised to find that I'm a domestic animal. Who the hell do they think washes my glass up every morning if there's no-one else there to do it? I cook, I sow, I reap, I . . .

While he does not see Elizabeth Smart, he does see the folded paper on the floor and recognizes it. Leaving the ironing board to collapse in a heap he crosses and picks it up and opens it out

Slightly rhyming verses for Jeff Bernard's fiftieth birthday, by Elizabeth Smart.

Smart   Wilde would have smiled
                 and been beguiled
                 and bright enough to know
                 that *you* had a better
                 Muse in tow
                 than he.

                 Could he see

the angelic emanations
from gutters where we
all fall, while
trying to pee,
and rise, or try to rise,
unwisely, in majesty?

Your subject is not mean,
who's up, who's in,
or jockeying for position
(what a dreary sin).
Funny but kind,
your subject is justly seen
as the inexhaustible one
of nude mankind.

Yourself, in fact, drinking,
amidst the alien corn,
and explaining the amazing
joke of being born.

Elizabeth Smart is lost in the shadows

Jeff sits, lights a cigarette, and thinks about her

Jeff It's terrible to think that dear Elizabeth got me my first job in journalism. We got drunk together one lunchtime and she took me back to her office at *Queen* magazine and said to the editor, "Give him a job." He did. Until then, I was a reasonably happy, sane stage-hand. She's dead now, like too many of my friends. God forgive you and rest in peace, Elizabeth. And if anybody writes to tell me you only get out of life what you put into it, I might just kill them.

He closes his eyes, cigarette in hand, and for a moment seems to be asleep. But then he opens them again

That was the most touching, but not the only poem I've had addressed to me.

Mistress With the crown of thorns I wear
Why do I need a prick like you?
If you choose to bugger off
It isn't going to spoil the view.

I've been put down by the best
And crucified by experts, dear,
And I really do not need
A friend like you to bend my ear.

You claim that generosity
Is something that I lack
May I suggest you've had from me
Much more than you gave back.

So don't think I'll mope and mourn
Because you tell me that we're through.
With the crown of thorns I wear
I sure don't need a prick like you.

But Jeff, lighted cigarette between his fingers, has gently nodded off

Jeffrey, I want to know who wrote that poem to you and why. Jeff?
Jeffrey! Oh—you make me sick!

CURTAIN

ACT II

The same. Perhaps an hour later

The light of dawn filters through the windows of the "Coach and Horses", highlighting the wisps of smoke from the chair or sofa which has been set on fire by Jeff's cigarette while he was asleep

Muttering oaths, he has been trying to extinguish the conflagration with a pair of old cricket flannels from his suitcase. He now acquires a soda siphon from the bar and applies it to the smouldering upholstery

Jeff (*muttering to himself*) This—is going to do—my reputation—no good—whatsoever ... Such as it is. How absurd. How ridiculously absurd ...

He surveys his flannels, which are badly charred, and tosses them aside

Which makes me a survivor, I suppose. A good friend of mine, Eva Johansen, used to say you can't get through life without a highly-developed sense of the absurd. She could well have been here now to recognize the absurdity of my situation, but one night she went to bed drunk with a lit cigarette in her hand and in her case she was taken seriously. How inconsiderate, Eva. Soon there'll be no-one left to drink with at all ... The rows we had, always in pubs. And if Norman or some other anxious landlord tried to intervene, she'd say with her winning smile——

Eva Oh, it's quite all right. This is a friend of mine and I'm just trying to explain to him what a stupid bastard he is.

Jeff Our longest standing row goes back to when I was living in the country and I asked her what she'd like for breakfast.

Eva A slice of cold, rare, roast beef and a glass of Tio Pepe, preferably chilled.

Jeff Why can't you have a fucking egg like anyone else, you flash cow?

Eva Because I'm not anyone else.

Jeff And she wasn't. One of these people she used to call "these people" approached her here in the *Coach and Horses* with a view to picking her up.

Bore Good-morning. Nice day.

Eva Your place or mine?

Jeff Exit frightened rabbit. Someone who did succeed in picking her up and became a close friend, one day said to her for some reason——

Friend You know, Eva, if I hadn't met you I think I would have taken up keeping bees.

Jeff He was ever after known as The Beekeeper and Eva said——
Eva The poor sod wanted to keep bees and he ended up with a hornet's
nest.
Jeff Some months before she set herself on fire she wrote to me and it was a
case of like calling to like.
Eva So I have no flat, no job, no lover, no income and as far as I can see no
prospects. Even my cat has left me. I keep sitting around expecting fear
and all I'm getting is exhilaration. Here I am, exulting in the clean dry air
of absolute selfishness, secure in the knowledge that there's nothing more
they can do to me. If it weren't so totally out of keeping with everything
I've been told, I'd say it could only be described as happiness.

Jeff crosses to the telephone and dials

Jeff Wake up Norman! . . . Engaged. At least that means he's stirring . . .
(*Replacing the receiver*) You won't begrudge me breakfast, will you.
Norman?

*Going round the bar he locates and plugs in an electric kettle, then forages for
food*

Now shall it be tea and bikkies, tea and vinegar-flavoured crisps, tea and
prawn crackers, tea and tortilla chips, tea and roasted peanuts or tea and
pork scratchings, and is it possible to boil an egg in an electric kettle? Tea
and bikkies, I think.

*He finds a square biscuit tin and struggles to open it. He is holding it upside
down and the tinful of biscuits cascades to the floor, leaving Jeff holding the lid*

Fuck.

*During the following, he produces the items named and lays them out on the
bar counter*

Now what was that trick Keith Waterhouse used to do on the dance floor
of the old *Establishment Club* with a biscuit tin lid and what else? A pint
glass of water. A matchbox. His right shoe. And a raw egg.

*He hobbles round to the front of the bar and, following his own directions, sets
up the trick, c, on the floor*

And what you do is you set the biscuit tin lid lip-side up squarely over the
pint glass, so. Then you make a funnel of the matchbox sleeve and you
place it on top of the lid, bang in the centre. Then you perch the raw egg
on the funnel and what you do then is, you give the biscuit-tin lid such an
almighty thwack with the heel of your shoe that it flies off across the room
and the egg plops into the glass. Or not, as the case may be. I've never seen
the trick done unsuccessfully, but Keith tells me that when it doesn't work
it's remarkable how great an area one little egg can splatter. He was in a
hotel once in Birmingham for some reason, and doing the egg trick in the
residents' lounge for some reason, and there was this young eighteen-
year-old snooker champion in the bar, very high on the success he'd just
had, so of course, he wanted to do the egg trick and he got Keith to show

him how it was done. Then he tried it himself and the egg caused two thousand poundsworth of damage to the décor. And just before he was thrown out of the hotel the young man asked Keith where'd he gone wrong, and Keith said——

Waterhouse I forgot to add that you've got to be at least fifty years old and pissed out of your brains.

Jeff Well, I'm fifty years old and that's not tonic water I've been drinking all night . . . (*He positions himself for the egg trick*) You need a good unsteady hand, Keith says. Here we go. One . . . two . . .

He does the egg trick which, it is to be hoped, works. If it does:

I wish I hadn't done that. I hate pub tricks. Next thing you know I'll be telling Irish jokes.

If it doesn't work (and the egg should be hard-boiled just in case):

Sorry about that, Norman. I was just about to scramble an egg for my breakfast when I saw your ugly mug leering at me from the doorway, and it slipped from my nerveless fingers . . .

He now sets up the ironing board and, during the following, proceeds to iron his clean shirt. Subsequently, he changes his shirt and socks. The set by now should be strewn with his possessions and look as if he has set up home in it

But if memory serves me right, which it doesn't very often, we were talking about racing. At times, I think it would save a lot of time and travelling expenses just to get up in the morning, shove fifty quid down the loo and pull the chain. But at other times I like to spin out the agony by going to the races. I once went to an evening meeting at Windsor, got absolutely arseholed, lost every penny in my pocket and had no idea how to get back to London after the last race. I was almost the only person left on the racecourse and, as I stood desolately in the car park, I suddenly saw this beautiful white Rolls Royce heading for the gate. I stood in its way and signalled it to stop. The owner, as suave as any film star, asked——

Rolls' Owner Yes, what can I do for you?

Jeff I said——

Rolls' Owner (*amused*) He said, "I'm pissed and potless. Please take me to the *Dorchester* immediately and buy me a drink."

Jeff I'd never seen him before and I've never seen him since, but he was absolutely charming. He recognized someone who'd done their bollocks and was feeling thirsty. He drove me straight to the American Bar of the *Dorchester* and stood me a huge one. We never introduced ourselves. He just filled me up then gave me my taxi fare back to Soho. And that's typical of what happens at the races. You wouldn't get it in a soccer stadium or at a cricket match. The racing world is stuffed with lunatics, criminals, idiots, charmers, bastards and exceptionally nice people. Like, for instance, Valentine Dyall, the actor—remember the *Man in Black* on radio?—who was responsible for a classic exchange in the Bankruptcy Court.

Recorder To what do you attribute your downfall, Mr Dyall?
Dyall Two and a half mile handicap hurdles, sir.
Jeff As for my own downfall, I attribute it to my parentage. I was sired by a scenic designer who was himself by a theatrical impresario out of an actress. My dam was an opera singer, who was by an itinerant pork butcher out of a gypsy. My father designed the Lyons Corner Houses, did you know that? And his son washed up in them. He also designed the entrance to the *Strand Palace Hotel* which was so brilliant it's now in the Victoria and Albert Museum. In any other country it'd still be outside the *Strand Palace*. He was an architect—well, he would be, wouldn't he? My mother was very beautiful. And she had style. She was once in court for non-payment of a debt—she must have taken after one of her sons—when she got into a slanging match with one of the lawyers. The judge intervened.
Judge If you continue to speak in that vein, Mrs Bernard, I shall have to commit you for contempt of court.
Mrs Bernard Make that *utter* contempt.
Jeff She wanted to turn me into an officer and a gentleman, but at the same time she was throwing occasional cocktail parties for musicians, actors, actresses and similar interesting riff-raff. It didn't take me long to see that they were all getting a little more fun out of life than the Latin master at my prep school, or the local grocer in Holland Park. At naval college I fell naturally into the company of secret Gold Flake smokers and cherry-brandy swiggers who got into trouble, and eventually the officer and gentleman idea was knocked on the head by my being asked to leave. The Captain of the college paid me the greatest backhanded compliment I've ever received.
Captain Dear Mrs Bernard, While I consider Jeffrey to be psychologically unsuitable for public-school life, I believe he has a great future as a seam bowler.
Jeff And with that reference I set out on the great journey of life in search of more trouble. I didn't have to look further than the racecourse.

Changing his socks, Jeff unearths another photograph, of himself with a trainer

(*With a reminiscent smile*) Of all the lunatics I've known in racing, one of the looniest was a brilliant trainer whose wife had triplets—two boys and a girl. One night, after his wife and kids had gone to bed, he was downstairs enjoying a gargle with a merry band of punting-mad Irishmen when he had a brilliant idea. He crept up to the nursery, came back with the triplets in his arms, and dumped them in a row on the sofa.

The Trainer, carrying the babies—represented by dolls wearing only nappies—enters and arranges them on a sofa

Trainer All right, gentlemen, now we're going to play Find the Lady. Watch me shuffle the babies. No bamboozling or trick babies involved, it is the quickness of the hand which deceives the eye. Come along, Jeffrey, you look a sportsman. Place your bet.

Jeff I'll take a fiver on the middle one.
Trainer Jeffrey bets that the lady is the middle one. Is he right or is he wrong?

He holds the right-hand baby aloft and whips down its nappy

Sorry, my friend, on this occasion you lose. Now, give the game another sporting try. Find the Lady. Now you see her and now you do not. (*Shuffling the babies in the manner of a three-card trickster*) I switch the babies so, and you place your bet. The quickness of the hand deceives the——

His Wife appears in her nightdress

Wife Would you put those triplets back where you found them, please?

The Trainer scoops up two of the babies and she the other one, and he shamefacedly follows her off

Jeff The true gambler will, of course, bet on anything and there's no cure. When there's nothing to bet on I sometimes worry quite seriously about going mad. In fact, another winter might do it. The long-range weather men say the athletes among us will be skating on the Thames come January and you know what that means, don't you? No racing.

Caspar, with a cat in his arms, passes through the pub

Caspar (*cryptically*) Not necessarily.
Jeff That thin dividing line people are so fond of referring to, the one between sanity and insanity, was breached by that bloke there, and an equally mad bugger known as Tom the copywriter, plus my good self, the last time we had a surfeit of snow and ice. Caspar, his name is. He works, or did work until he was fired for spending too long in the betting shop, in one of the foreign embassies. Not exactly a career diplomat, but what's a career when there's racing at Doncaster.

Caspar moves out, stroking the cat

(*Confidentially*) Caspar's wife left him after he told her, in a moment of intoxication and great frankness, that in his considered opinion, when it came to who had the strongest hold on his affections, his wife or the great Italian racehorse Ribot, Ribot won by a furlong. So there he was, living all alone in this enormous flat opposite Battersea Park with his two cats, Keir Hardy and George Lansbury—because he was something of a socialist was Caspar—when it began to piss down with snow.

Caspar and Tom enter from opposite directions, both reading the "Sporting Life"

Tom Disaster. All racing cancelled.
Caspar Not necessarily.
Jeff For three weeks we fidgeted here in the pub, re-living the glories of our past wins and near misses, nigh desperate for a horse to lose our money

on. Then, on the twenty-second day of the great cold spell, Caspar walked
in and said——

Caspar Who fancies coming racing tonight?

Jeff Where? Australia or California?

Caspar Battersea.

Tom There's been no dog racing at Battersea for a month.

Caspar Not dog racing, my friend. Cat racing.

Jeff (*narrating*) When I spoke of going mad, I didn't necessarily mean I
would be the first in our little group to crack . . . (*To Caspar*) Cat racing.

Caspar Round at my place.

Tom That'd be a flat race, of course?

Caspar Normally yes, but since we're in the middle of the National Hunt
season I've had to build a hurdle course. Four jumps, and it's a good forty
feet from the starting post at the kitchen end of the passage to the front
door. So we get a run for our money.

*We are by now transported to Caspar's flat downstage. The "course" is
assumed to be up the aisle of the auditorium*

Jeff What are the odds?

Caspar Evens Keir Hardie, three to one the field.

Tom Both under starter's orders, are they?

Caspar Well put it this way, Tom. I haven't fed these cats for two days.
Now, I'm going to place a saucer of tinned salmon here by the front door,
give them a sniff of it, bring them back to the kitchen and then—they're
off!

Tom But they're not.

Caspar Not yet they're not—hold Keir Hardie. It's a seven thirty meeting,
isn't it?

Jeff (*narrating*) Course it is—and it's only seven twenty-nine. You've got to
do these things right. (*To Caspar*) George Lansbury looks a goer. I'll have
a pound to win.

Caspar and Tom are now crouching, holding their imaginary cats

Tom The same on this bugger.

Caspar And—let him go, Tom—they're off!

*Jeff, Tom and Caspar watch the race—Jeff in silence, the other two urging the
animals on*

Tom | Come on, Keir Hardie. Come on—you can do it, Keir
        (*together*) | Hardie—come on, my son!
Caspar | Jump, you bastards, jump!

Jeff (*narrating*) Keir Hardie by three lengths. While he and the runner-up
attacked their tinned salmon, Caspar, Tom and I retired to the sitting-
room, hereinafter referred to as the Steward's Room, to discuss the next
meeting.

Tom *I've* got a moggy I wouldn't mind entering, Caspar. A little tabby
called Samantha.

Caspar Ah—a filly.

Tom Two-year-old.

Jeff (*to Tom*) When can I see her gallops?

Tom Mornings, in the back yard.

Jeff Form?

Tom She's never been in a cat race. But with the dog next door behind her, she's a goer.

Caspar She's entered.

Jeff (*narrating*) Samantha missed the first race, being delayed on the tube due to incident on line at Earl's Court. Some poor frozen sod threw himself under the train in a last desperate effort to get warm, I shouldn't wonder. Keir Hardie once again romped it and once again I went down on George Lansbury whose form I was led to believe had improved. I said to Caspar: This is not going to be a bundle of laughs if the favourite's going to win every race.

Caspar You're right. When Samantha turns up we'll make it a handicap race.

Jeff How do you propose to do that?

Caspar With the weights off the kitchen scales.

Jeff Of course. (*Narrating*) We agreed that if horses get three pounds for a length then cats should get an ounce for a length. Keir Hardie finished up carrying three ounces, stuck to his back with Sellotape. Then Tom turned up with Samantha, this evil-looking tabby outsider. Samantha was very much on edge and a few years in the racing game have made me easily suspicious. I was even more suspicious when Tom asked, all nonchalant——

Tom Anyone care to lay four fivers on her?

Jeff We declined and I had a quid at threes on George Lansbury, who I was convinced was improving with every race.

Caspar Under starter's orders.

The three of them crouch with the imaginary cats, releasing them at the cry of:

And they're off!

Tom (*as a racing commentator*) And it's Keir Hardie away first followed by Lansbury then Samantha. Samantha taking the lead, over the first hurdle, under the second and it's Samantha way in front and the rest nowhere as Samantha grabs the tinned salmon and tries to hurl herself through the fucking door. What a race! Samantha first, Lansbury second, Keir Hardy still struggling to the post.

Caspar Could I have a word with you, Tom?

Jeff (*narrating*) You'd have thought Caspar was Lord Derby, the way he carried on. He actually pulled a red handkerchief out of his pocket, which I correctly guessed to be cat racing's equivalent of the red flag at Newmarket or Epsom, denoting a Steward's Enquiry.

Caspar You doped that cat, didn't you, Tom?

Tom What are you talking about?

Caspar Come on, you gave it a Dexedrine or some sort of pep pill, didn't you?

Tom You'd better watch what you're saying, Caspar. Nobody accuses me of cat-doping.

Caspar Well *I'm* accusing you, friend.

Tom Right. Come outside.

They march angrily out

Jeff And that was the end of cat racing. Or was it? A few weeks later, chancing to wake up in Battersea, for reasons now lost in the mists of time, I was walking home through the park when who should I bump into but Caspar.

Caspar has reappeared, with a pair of binoculars focussed on some distant object

What are you doing, Caspar?

Caspar Cantering Keir Hardie.

Jeff Oh, yes?

Caspar We could be in for a very hot summer. A drought, in fact. In which case, the going could be so hard that racing might be cancelled again. You never know, Jeff.

Jeff You never do. (*Softly: observing the cat in the distance*) Just wait till he gets the sun on his back.

Lighting a cigarette and enduring a coughing fit, he crosses to the phone and dials. After listening for a while, he slams down the receiver

Oh, for God's sake! Talk about waiting for Godot—now the bugger's not there. He must have gone to Smithfield to select the savoury mince. Or New Covent Garden for today's dawn-plucked crop of frozen peas . . . (*Rubbing his chin*) I need a shave. If I'd stayed in the French Pub last night, none of this would have happened. But I was driven out of the French Pub, wasn't I, by a man who walked up to me and said——

Bore D'you remember Peter the Pole who worked in the dirty bookshop in St Anne's Court? You know, the bloke whose father is an ear, nose and throat surgeon in Warsaw? Well anyway, he's just moved to Hounslow.

Jeff There's no answer to that. Not only do I not know Peter the Pole, have never even heard of him, nor care greatly how his father scrapes a living, I also have very little time for a man who moves to Hounslow and wouldn't trust him an inch. So I repaired to the *Coach and Horses*, to ponder the meaning of life and man's incredible ascent from the discovery of fire and the invention of the wheel to the ability to move to Hounslow, only to find myself confronted by Norman's unfortunate mother, who whispered in my ear——

Norman's Mother I bet you didn't know my grandfather had an umbrella shop in Gower Street.

Jeff Oddly enough the possibility of Norman's mother's grandfather having had an umbrella shop in Gower Street had never crossed my seething brain, although God knows I'm a broad-minded man. Well, after a short but emotional discussion on the subject of the eighteen ninety umbrella boom in Gower Street I felt in need of a strictly medicinal drink, and in the hour or so it took to get served, it suddenly clicked. I was in the middle of some dreadful plot. These mad utterances were codes or ciphers like the Thirty-nine Steps or the Five Orange Pips or the Dancing Men. Obviously, I was to meet a man with a Polish accent in Hounslow who would give me a message to deliver to an ear, nose and throat specialist in an umbrella shop in Gower Street. Nothing so extraordinary about that after all, is there?

Jeff fishes out an electric razor from his belongings. With it he unearths a dog-eared copy of "Vogue"

(*Shaving*) Now what the fuck am I doing with last month's *Vogue*? Perhaps I'm supposed to be writing something for them. Who's in and who's out in the drinking clubs. No Knickers Joyce is in, Herpes Henry is out, in fact barred for life. Or perhaps I'm in it. Jeffrey Bernard seen throwing up over a friend on Ladies' Day at Royal Ascot . . . Well, the sun ought to be well over the yardarm somewhere in the world by now. Time for a Bloody Mary. (*Mixing it with care*) The merit of these things is that you can persuade yourself you're having breakfast, and a healthy one at that. Though it's possible to overdo the health angle. A bloke I know had fourteen healthy breakfasts on the trot and what with one thing leading to another didn't arrive home until six the next morning when he was totally legless and bursting for a pee. Falling out of his taxi, he was just about to urinate in desperation against the offside rear wheel, which like all of us he erroneously believed to be legal, when a dear old couple hove into sight very possibly on their way to early morning Mass. Some modicum of decorum prompted our man to do the decent thing and so he zipped up and bounded up the steps to his front door which he attempted to unlock. Unfortunately, his keys not being magnetic, he was unable to make contact. One knows the problem.

Having mixed his Bloody Mary, he now attempts to pick it up but his hand is too shaky. He tries to steady it by gripping his wrist with his other hand:

(*Managing the manoeuvre*) Health hint. A good cure for shaky hands: grip the glass very firmly . . . So, our man can't get his key in the lock and by now he's at his wits' end — no great distance to travel. There's only one thing to do. He inserts his member through the letter-box and proceeds to relieve himself. Now. It so happens that at this precise moment his landlord, a naturally angry man who has been trying to evict our hero for some time, is coming down the staircase with the not unreasonable intention of taking his dog for a walk. You can imagine his and Fido's bemusement when confronted, not with the terror of a buff envelope thudding through the letter-box, but with our man's cascading member. The hound backed away snarling and steaming, the landlord — one can only imagine — clasped his fluttering heart and our man politely turned his head to say good-morning to the churchgoing pair he'd originally tried to avoid offending. There has to be a moral there somewhere, but I'm damned if I can work out what it is. Cheers.

My own worst experience in the same direction was waking up in the
bottom drawer of an Edwardian wardrobe dying to spend a penny.
Imagine trying to open a drawer from the inside and you'll appreciate my
predicament. But however desperate, I would never have done it through
the keyhole. I mean, just imagine—if that dog had been of a more savage
disposition. The eyes water just to think about it . . .

He freshens up his Bloody Mary with another vodka

I need this, because I'm reluctantly reminded of the man in the paper who
chopped off his own chopper and threw it in the fire so he could devote the
rest of his life to God without any further distractions. With his wife's
blessing, wouldn't you know—they'd been discussing it for twelve years.
She was probably a *Guardian* reader after her Jill'll Fix It badge. But what
I want to know is why did the wretched man pick on his perfectly
harmless cock? Surely he must have realized that sex is all in the mind and
that his dangler was merely his solo instrument in a far bigger concerto
than you or I will ever comprehend. I mean, if I wanted to devote the rest
of my life to any one thing at all without being distracted I'd cut off my
head. And another thing. Why dispose of the blackballed ex-member on
the fire? What on earth does he think wastepaper baskets are for? And
then of course I can't help wondering what this couple's sex life must have
been like during their twelve years of disarmament talks. Pretty tentative,
I should think. The fact that God didn't intervene in the matter proves my
theory that He is a woman after all—probably another *Guardian* reader.
And who took the initiative? What a mug! I mean, it so happens I don't
have a wife at the present moment but if there chanced to be a Mrs
Bernard Mark Five and she took to chatting me up on certain lines, I'd be
more than suspicious.

Fifth Wife So why won't you?
Jeff Why won't I what?
Fifth Wife Cut it off.
Jeff Why should I?
Fifth Wife You never do anything for me these days. You never do the
shopping, you won't wash up, you don't ever bring me in a cup of tea in
bed. I know you're a lazy, idle, selfish brute, Jeff, but for heaven's sake—is
it such a big thing?
Jeff (*reflecting*) Not really, no.
Fifth Wife Then cut it off!
Jeff No.
Fifth Wife Please? Pretty please? For me, darling. Come on—just be a love
and cut it off.
Jeff (*narrating again*) Do you know, there's a possible TV sitcom in this.
Fifth Wife Then I shall just have to cut it off for you!
Jeff Or possibly a one-off video nasty. Not, despite these occasional
nightmares, that there's the slightest chance of there ever being a fifth Mrs
Bernard. I've learned very slowly that for a boozer on my scale, marriage
is impossible. Drink is the other woman. (*Displaying his shaking hands*)
With the evidence of the affair only too visible.

A Doctor approaches him significantly and helps him into a dressing-gown

Doctor Come along, Mr Bernard. There's only one place for you.

Jeff suffers himself to be put to bed

Jeff At last, after years of trying, I'd finally landed the spring double. Pneumonia *and* pleurisy. So here I was back in the same hospital where I was first shown the yellow card in December nineteen sixty-five. But this was the first time I'd ever been in hospital for something that wasn't self-inflicted and that made it seem a little unfair. I mean, they didn't *conscript* kamikaze pilots, did they, Nurse?

Nurse Eat your mince.

Jeff They put me in the Ellen Terry Ward just down the corridor from the Alfred Tennyson. The nurses were nice. It's not always the case and some of them can be right nutters, but then look who they've got to contend with. The patients never change. They must be provided by some sort of agency. There's always a Paisley dressing-gown sort of bloke with a jar of Tiptree jam in his locker and trouble with what he calls "the old waterworks". There's always someone dying in a resigned sort of way . . . Otherwise it's the usual cast – *Sun* readers to a man, they stare vacantly at Hungarian children's cartoons on the box all afternoon, occasionally coughing and farting. And to think that's going to be the curtain-down scene for most of us. And the menu for the last supper will be brown Windsor soup and minced beef with cabbage and boiled potatoes.

A Nurse approaches with a syringe

Nurse Just a little prick, Jeffrey.

Jeff They always say that. It's their joke. Little pricks please little minds, don't they, darling?

Nurse Eat your prunes.

She injects him. During the following he becomes progressively more tired

Jeff Needless to say, in this situation one's thoughts tend to drift towards the Grim Reaper. There's a dreadful fellow in the French Pub who once tried to make a book on who would be next in Soho for the last jump and he made me five to four favourite, so he was pleased to tell me. But the long shots keep coming in and although I'm only too delighted to survive, it's a lousy race to have been entered for. Eva. Frank Norman. John Le Mes. Sean Lynch who ran *Gerry's Club*. Dennis Shaw even. And dear old Jeremy Madden-Simpson, rechristened by Eva Jeremy Madman-Simpleton, certainly won't be walking into the *Coach and Horses* come opening time. Old? He hadn't turned forty. We first got really friendly after I broke a bone in my right hand on him one night in the French Pub – for what reason neither of us could remember, but he'd say——

Jeremy But if you can't hit a friend, who can you hit?

Jeff Once when I was at death's door in this very hospital he used to visit me every evening with a croissant for tomorrow's breakfast. When a piss artist takes time off during licensed hours to visit you then you know you've got a friend. Sometimes, when I wonder whether this interval on earth might be just a bit of nonsense, I think about all those friends who've gone. And the lunchtime sessions in the *Coach* when they were all still here were worth all the trappings of all the success stories you've ever heard, and I'd rather keep down with the likes of Jeremy than up with the Joneses. I do worry about my own wretched mortality, though. Shuffling off this mortal coil it seems as though we're in a queue that's shuffling along towards a sort of bus stop. "Who's next?" "No, sorry chum. You were before me." Maybe the party could go on, though. Different premises and no closing time. A kind of celestial and sterilized *Colony Room Club* ...

He has fallen asleep, a lit cigarette inevitably between his fingers

The Doctor enters and shakes him awake

Doctor Mr Bernard? Mr Bernard! Are you trying to set the hospital on fire?
Jeff (*sleepily*) Just the bed, Doctor. I have no territorial ambitions.
Doctor I'm discharging you, Mr Bernard. But I want you to do nothing at all for the next two or three weeks.
Jeff That shouldn't be too difficult.
Doctor By which I mean you're to stay at home.
Jeff Yes, Doctor.

Discarding his dressing-gown, he heads straight for the bar and pours himself a drink

Home is where the heart is ... I wonder if Norman would let me live here—I mean considering I *do* live here he might as well be charging rent. What did once strike me, though, is that I could hang about in the window of the Reject Shop in the Kings Road. I mean I could actually get bought by someone quite nice. I see myself being bought by a tarty blonde who'd show me off to her friends in a sleazy afternoon drinking club in Shepherds Market ...
Tart Yes, I bought him in the Reject Shop in Chelsea. Not bad for twenty-five quid, including VAT. He couldn't get it up, mind you, when I first got him home, but it's amazing what a couple of stiff vodkas will do. Have another, ducks.
Jeff I can think of quite a number of personalities who could further their wilting careers in the Reject Shop. For instance——

The telephone rings shrilly and unexpectedly. Jeff stares at it. As it continues to ring, he approaches the phone warily, then gingerly picks it up

Coach and Horses? ... Norman! What the fuck do you mean, what am I fucking doing here? ... How the fuck did you *know* I was fucking here? ... Oh, I see ... The cleaning lady—no, she's not arrived yet. Any messages? ... It's a long story, Norman. No, in fact it's a short story. I fell asleep in the bog and why the hell don't you call "Time Gents, Please" in the gents? I mean I would have thought there'd be some kind of legal requirement under the Landlords' Liability Act. Oh, and talking of the

law, Norman, I appear to have caned the best part of a bottle of vodka.
Does that count as drinking after hours, I mean given the circumstances?
I'll tell you one thing, Norman, the service was a bloody sight faster than
it usually is. If you made this Britain's first self-service pub you'd
quadruple the takings overnight . . . Yes, Norman . . . No, Norman . . . I
owe you for vodka, one tomato juice, a dash of Worcester sauce, one tea
bag, a slightly cracked egg, oh, and a tin of biscuits which unfortunately
became spilled . . . What do you mean, what have I been up to all night? I
have been sitting here quietly nursing my drink and contemplating the
meaning of life. It's all going to change, Norman, starting tomorrow. . . .
All right then, if you insist – to-fucking-day. Now how long are you going
to be? . . . Of course I won't move till you get here– I'm hardly in a
position to move, am I? . . . No, I won't touch anything, Norman, I'll just
get on with my packing. . . . My packing. It's another long story, mate.
Just get off your arse and get down here . . .

*He replaces the telephone. During the following he re-packs his scattered
belongings*

He's coming. I've never seen Norman at seven in the morning before– it
should be a fascinating if grisly sight. Come to that, he's never seen me at
seven in the morning. People who have say I'm not at my best, though
they do generously add that I'm not at my worst, either.

Jeff now picks up the bundle of letters which he tossed down earlier

(*Leafing through them*) Dearest Jeff . . . Jeff dear . . . Dear Jeff . . .

*He tosses the letters into his bag one by one as the Mistress appears and he
hears fragments from the correspondence as it progresses*

Mistress So looking forward to next weekend . . .
        Wasn't last weekend fun . . .
        Still missing you terribly . . .
        So looking forward to Friday . . .
        I waited and waited – where were you? . . .
        We must try harder . . .
        I'm tired of your excuses . . .
        We can't go on like this . . .
        I must have been mad to think it would work . . .
        It's goodbye, Jeffrey. This time I really mean it. You've gone too
        far.
Jeff And I make her sick. There's a bloke I know in what's left of Fleet
Street who plans to sink his redundancy money in an establishment to be
called the *This Time I Really Mean It Hotel*, specially designed for people
who've just walked out on, or been walked out on by their spouses. You
could check in at any hour of the night without luggage – there'd be a
razor, toothbrush and change of clothes on every pillow along with the
after-dinner Valium wrapped in tinfoil. And there'd be a twenty-four-
hour bar known as the *Gone Too Far Bar* where you could drink yourself
silly. And every night they'd have an Unhappy Hour when the drinks

would cost double and you could tell the barman your troubles . . . I wish he'd get on with it — I'd book a permanent suite.

Towards the end of the bundle of letters he finds a dry-cleaning bill

The things one keeps. An old dry-cleaning bill. To removing tartare sauce from top pocket . . . (*Screwing the paper up and tossing it away*) I've no memory of that whatsoever but I do have unhappy memories of tartare sauce in general. I woke up in the *Groucho Club* one day thinking I'd gone blind. I was scared shitless. It turned out I'd been resting my head on a grilled turbot and I had tartare sauce all over my reading glasses . . .

Now turning up a buff envelope

This is good. A demand from the Inland Revenue for one thousand seven hundred and sixty pounds. It's to be hoped they're pulling my pisser. One hundred and seventy quid would just about crucify me but one thousand seven hundred and sixty is a joke and utterly beyond me. . . . There's always suicide, of course. So many of us around here have contemplated it at one time or another that Dave in the French Pub once had the idea of us all hiring a coach and driving it over Beachy Head. Fifty-two seats only. Book now to avoid disappointment.

He has now completed his packing

I'd better have the one.

As he pours himself a drink, there is a clinking sound from without

(*Looking towards the outer door*) Norman . . . ? No, it's the milkman. Always the signal to the law-abiding citizen to be making tracks home . . . if he had a home to go to . . .

He moves back to his belongings and fastens up his suitcase, then sits down, nursing his vodka

What the hell — this *is* home: — sitting by the bedside of dying Soho holding her hand but wondering wouldn't it be kinder to switch off the life-support system . . . (*Contemplating his drink*) What an amazing jemmy to the door of the mind is a few large vodkas . . .

1st Friend Let's start a club for people who've been barred from all the others. Instead of throwing members out, we'll throw them in.
1st Girl You don't bring me flowers any more.
2nd Friend Don't worry, Jeff. Give it me back when you get a win.
2nd Girl Couldn't you have telephoned?
3rd Friend Now if I put you in a cab will you promise not to fall out the other door?
3rd Girl You only get out of life what you put into it.
4th Friend Fancy a spot of cat racing, Jeff?
4th Girl You're a mean, alcoholic, diabetic little prick.
Jeff And?
4th Girl You make me sick.

Jeff, far away, sits in his chair, smoking

Elizabeth Smart appears

Smart   But you're never snide
                   and you never hurt,
                   and you wouldn't want to win
                   on a doctored beast,
                   and, anyway, the least
                   of your pleasures
                   resides in paltry measures.

                   So guard, great joker God, please guard
                   this great Bernard . . .
                   Let him be known
                   for the prince of men he is,
                   a master at taking out of
                   himself and us the piss.

Jeff (*simply*) Thank you.

He stirs as he sees a shadow flit past a window

The bugger's here at last.

He stands, picks up his suitcase and carrier bags, and faces the outer door

Come on, Godot . . . ! (*Raising his voice*) And I meant what I said, Norman! It's all going to change, starting to-fucking-day. It's new leaf time! From now on it'll be gin instead of vodka, Capstan Full Strength instead of Senior Service and the French Pub instead of the *Coach and Horses* . . . (*To himself, softly, as a key scrapes in the door lock*) And life does go on, whatever proof there may be to the contrary. Last week . . . last week I had an erection. I was so amazed I took its photograph. Life after death! What more do you want? Come on, Norman!

The outer door opens as——
                        ——the CURTAIN *falls*

FURNITURE AND PROPERTY LIST

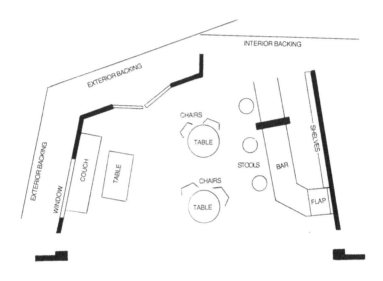

ACT I

On stage: Pub tables. *On them:* ashtrays. *On one:* bottle of wine, 2 glasses
Chairs
Chaise longue or sofa
Bar. *On it:* telephone, ashtrays, soda siphon, bottle of Worcestershire sauce, bottle of water.
Under it: bottle of vodka, bottle of tomato juice, glasses (including a pint glass), hard-boiled egg, box of matches, square biscuit tin containing biscuits, tin of teabags, mug.
Behind it: two carrier bags containing framed photograph of Lester Piggott, bundle of letters with dry-cleaning bill and buff envelope, framed photographs of **Jeff** with various ladies, framed photograph of the **Mistress**, pair of tortoiseshell-backed hairbrushes, various framed photographs, cassette tapes, electric (practical) razor with dog-eared copy of *Vogue*; suitcase containing clean, crumpled shirt with folded page from the *Spectator* in the pocket, pair of socks, framed photograph of **Jeff** with a trainer
Shelves. *On them:* glasses, various bottles with optic fittings, electric kettle and powerpoint (practical)
Bar stools. *On one:* copy of *The Times*

                        Clock on wall
                        Jeff's jacket on floor
Off stage: Copy of the *Sporting Life* **(Nurse)**
                        Ironing board and iron **(Jeff)**
Personal: **Jeff:** Senior Service cigarettes, matches
                        Old Reliable: pipe, tobacco, matches
                        Customs Officers: notebooks, pens
                        Customs Investigator: identity card

ACT II

Set: Pair of charred flannel trousers (for **Jeff**)

Off stage: Three dolls with nappies **(Trainer)**
                        Cat **(Caspar)**
                        Copies of the *Sporting Life* **(Caspar** and **Tom)**
                        Pair of binoculars **(Caspar)**
                        Dressing-gown **(Doctor)**
                        Syringe **(Nurse)**

Personal: **Caspar:** red handkerchief in pocket

LIGHTING PLOT

Practical fittings required: wall lights

ACT I

To open: Black-out

ACT II

To open: Dawn light filtering through windows, all practicals and covering spots on

EFFECTS PLOT

ACT I

Cue 1   **Jeff:** "... deliciously blaming herself."   (Page 12)
          Sound of screeching brakes

Cue 2   **Jeff:** "... to an old, reliable friend."   (Page 13)
          Bring up Mahler recording; fade when ready

Cue 3   **Jeff:** "... on Radio Three any day."   (Page 15)
          Snatch of Der Rosenkavalier; *fade when ready*

ACT II

Cue 4   To open   (Page 23)
          Wisps of smoke from chair or sofa

Cue 5   **Jeff:** "For instance — "   (Page 34)
          Telephone

Cue 6   **Jeff** pours himself a drink   (Page 36)
          Clinking sound from outside

Lightning Source UK Ltd.
Milton Keynes UK
UKOW06f1144250815

257488UK00013B/172/P